Early Learning

Sticker Activity

Animals

priddy books
big ideas for little people

goose

turkey

duck

rooster

Who says neigh?

goats

pig

donkey

horse

farm

chicks

Who says moo?

cow

Who says baaa?

sheep

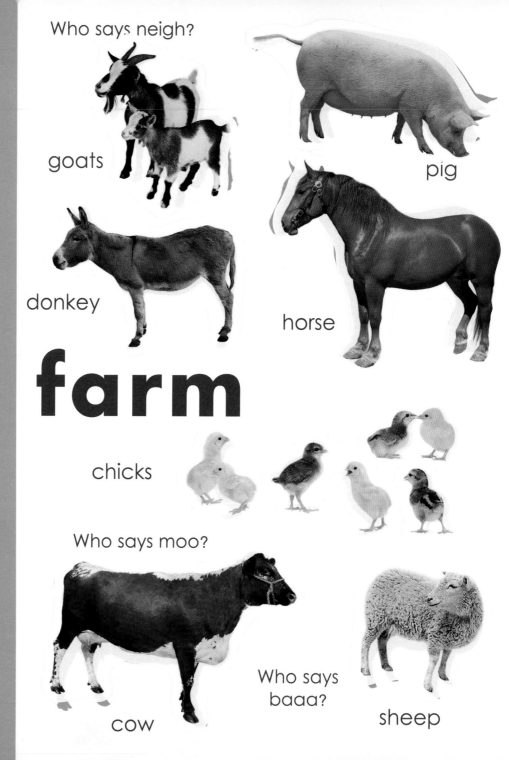

Which pet has feathers?

kittens

parakeet

pets

dog

Do you have any of these pets?

rabbit

chinchilla

tortoise

goldfish

guinea pigs

lorikeet

cockatoo

macaw

parrot

Can you match the moms to their babies?

dog

giraffe

elephant

cat

gosling

tiger cub

babies

Which babies live on a farm?

foal

puppy

kitten

lamb

Which baby has a wooly coat?

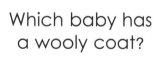

elephant calf

giraffe calf

 frog

 camel

 deer

Which animal has two humps?

 porcupine

 rhinoceros

 panda

Can you find the animal with very sharp prickles?

wild

gorilla

 lioness

Which animal has scales?

 zebra

 snake

 raccoon

 tiger

Can you find the odd one out?

butterfly

butterfly

scorpion

butterfly

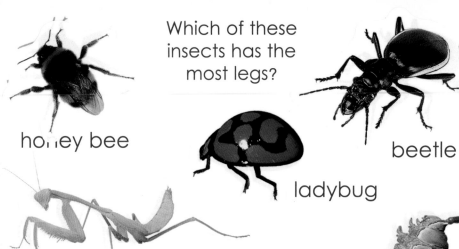

honey bee

Which of these insects has the most legs?

beetle

ladybug

praying mantis

How many insects can you count?

caterpillar

ants

minibeasts

stick insect

millipede

fly

spider

Can you find a round fish with spikes?

orca

puffertish

How many yellow sea creatures can you see?

dolphin

sea

seahorse

shark

Which of these sea creatures can go on land?

sea lion

yellow tang fish

Which triangle has the most fish?

two fish

four fish

three fish

one fish

Can you match these colors to the birds?

blue

red

brown

pink

owl

Can you spot the bird with pink feathers?

pheasant

swan

kookaburra

birds

Which of these birds cannot fly?

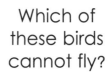
flamingo

penguin

peacock

eagle

egret

toucan

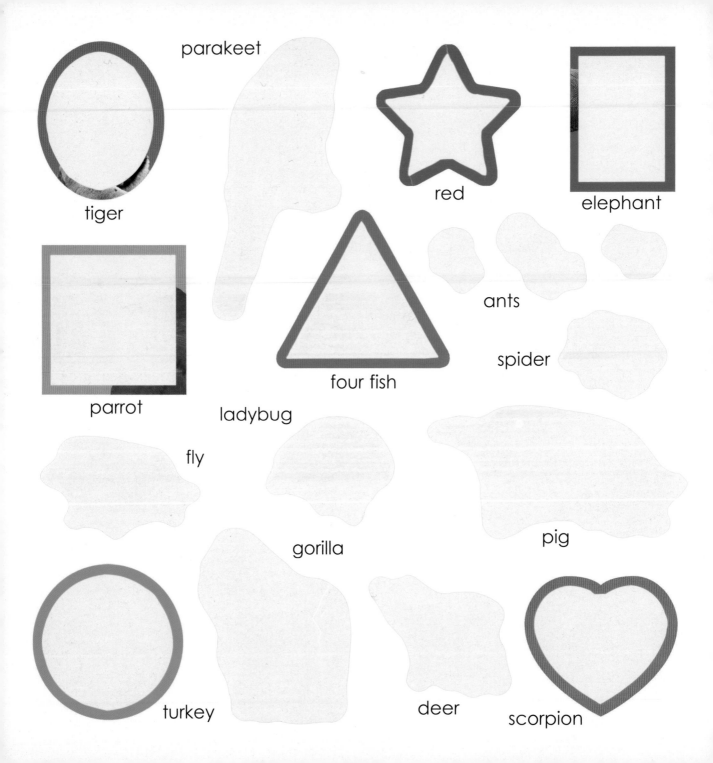

parakeet

red

elephant

tiger

ants

spider

parrot

four fish

ladybug

fly

gorilla

pig

turkey

deer

scorpion

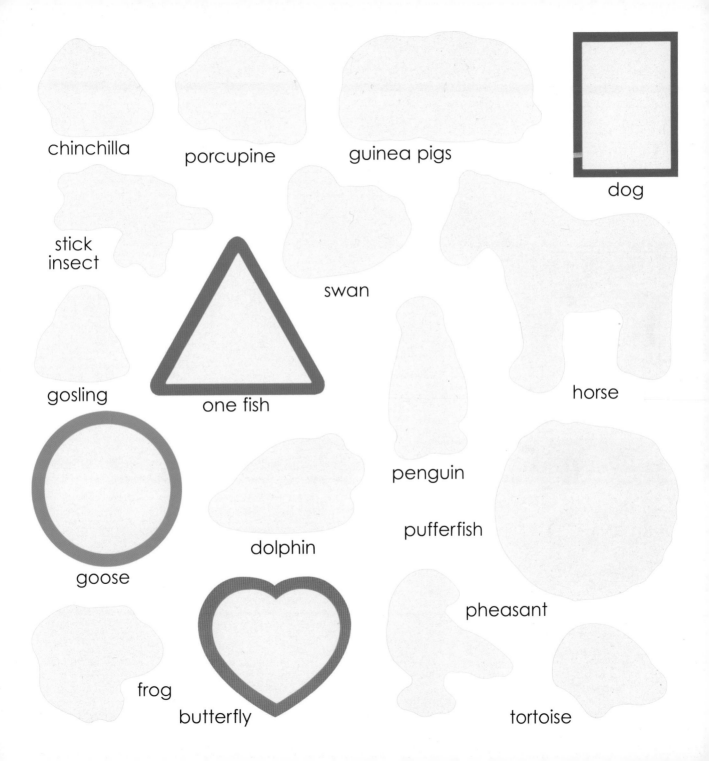

chinchilla

porcupine

guinea pigs

dog

stick
insect

swan

horse

gosling

one fish

penguin

goose

dolphin

pufferfish

pheasant

frog

butterfly

tortoise

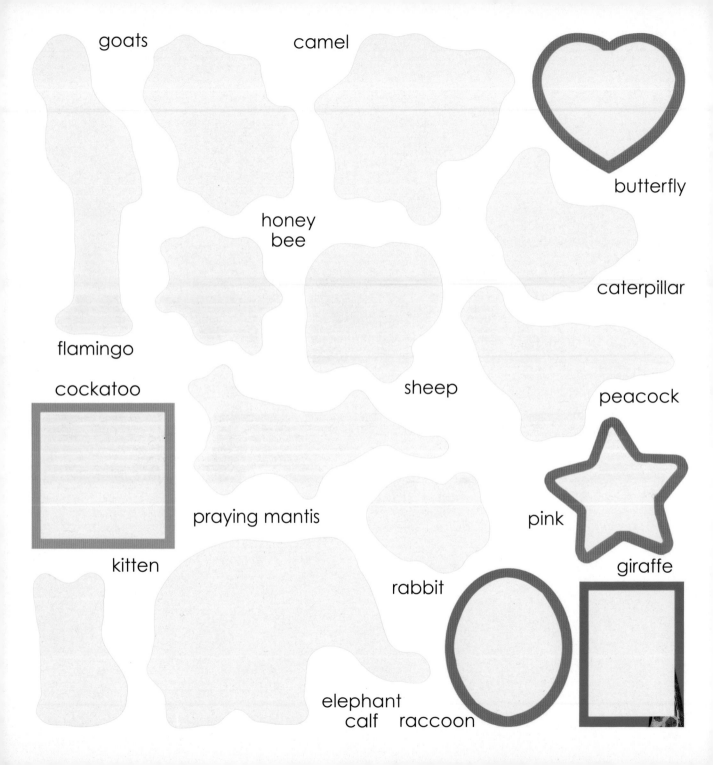

goats

camel

butterfly

honey
bee

caterpillar

flamingo

cockatoo

sheep

peacock

praying mantis

pink

kitten

rabbit

giraffe

elephant
calf   raccoon

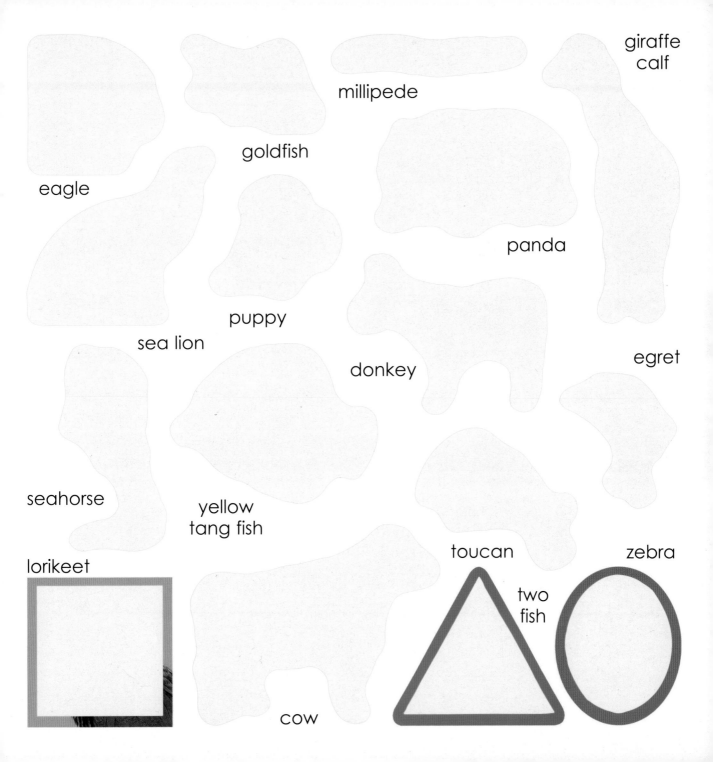

giraffe
calf

millipede

goldfish

eagle

panda

puppy

sea lion

donkey

egret

seahorse

yellow
tang fish

toucan

zebra

lorikeet

two
fish

cow

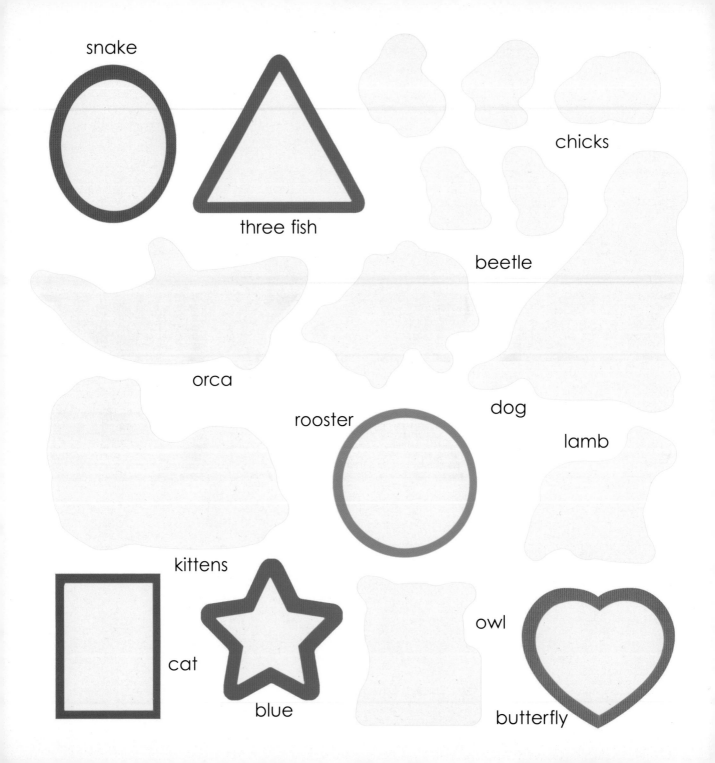

snake

three fish

chicks

beetle

orca

dog

rooster

lamb

kittens

cat

blue

owl

butterfly

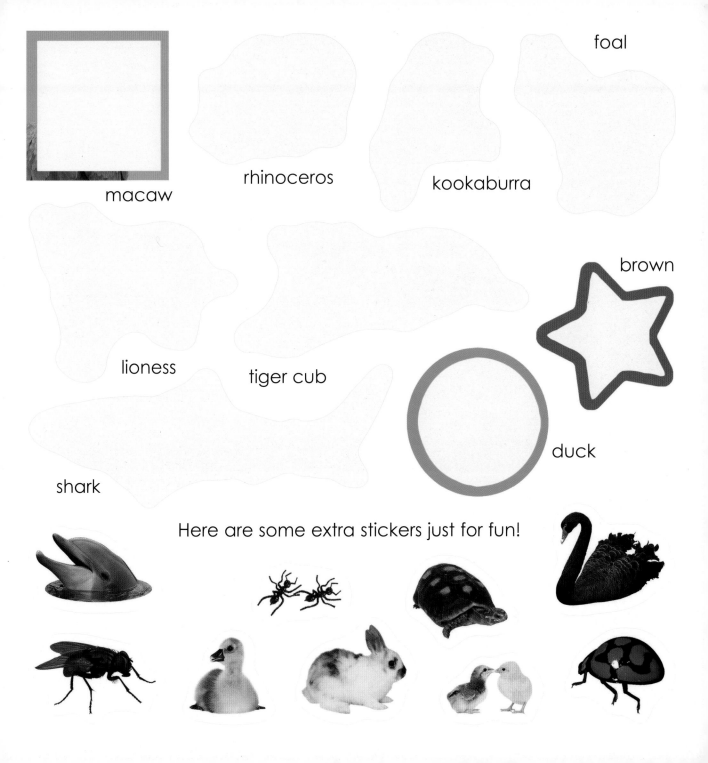

macaw

rhinoceros

kookaburra

foal

lioness

tiger cub

brown

duck

shark

Here are some extra stickers just for fun!

rabbits

parakeet

goldfish

guinea pig

dog

goat

sheep

rooster

hen

cow

calf

horse

foal

piglets

pig

frog

snake

crocodile

monkey

giraffe

elephant

tiger

shark

dolphin

fish

orcas

turtle

seahorse

octopus

geese

kingfisher   heron

swan

eagle

parrot

ostrich

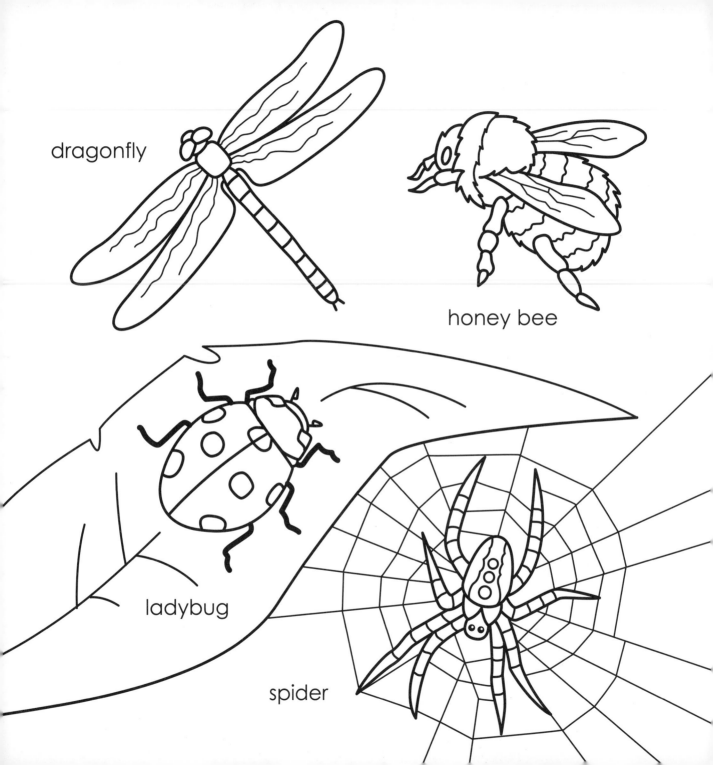

dragonfly

honey bee

ladybug

spider

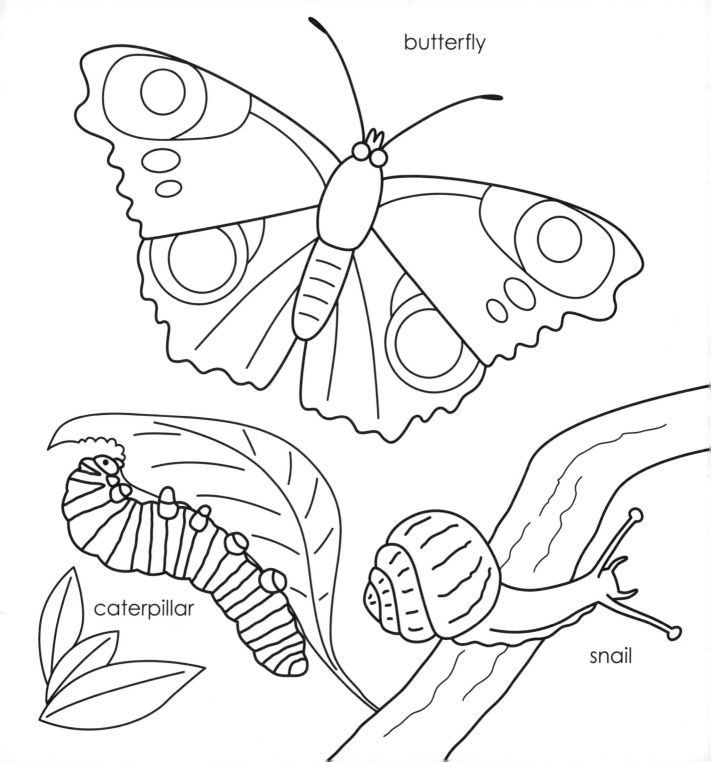

butterfly

caterpillar

snail

Draw your own picture here.

Drawn by

....